A Bi
of tne Hopewell

Charlotte L. Stiverson

Illustrated by Kati Aitken

WRINKLED ROCK PUBLISHING

BAINBRIDGE • OHIO

Dedicated to –

My family and Ohio's prehistoric families.
Charlotte Stiverson

*Native Americans and the people of the First
Nations in the hope of keeping their stories
alive for future generations.*
Kati Aitken

A Bird's Eye View of the Hopewell

Charlotte L. Stiverson

Copyright ©2019 • Wrinkled Rock Publishing

Book Design by Aaron Keirns

ISBN 978-0-578-61377-2

"**W**hat is happening?" Rabbit whispered to Squirrel.

THUMP, THUD, THUMP. The drum kept beat as the people swirled around the fire.

While Rabbit and Squirrel sat engrossed in the movement, they were startled by a dark shadow cast by the setting sun. Both glanced up to see the great horned owl swoop down and land nearby. Owl, whose sharp hearing had picked up on Rabbit's question, came to shed light on the activities from a bird's eye view.

Growing up together at Mound City, Owl, Rabbit, and Squirrel's lifelong friendship created an understanding and trust. They looked out for each other in an environment that sometimes threatened smaller animals, and they survived by sharing their talents with one another. Owl was respected by her furry friends for her wisdom, helpfulness, and keen observation skills, and now they listened intently as she shed light on what was happening around them.

"You are witnessing what appears to be a Hopewell burial ceremony," hooted Owl.

"So, it's not a war call for others to join in a fight?" whispered Rabbit, relieved with this discovery.

"Certainly not!" replied Owl. "The Hopewell people are known for having a peaceful community, perhaps because their society is equal and decisions are made collectively. While leaders may obtain status through accomplishments, they work as hard as everyone else, live in the same type of houses, and eat the same type of food."

"I feel safer now knowing that this is a celebration," sighed Rabbit.

"In the ceremony you are watching," Owl continued, "there are all types of people and many of them are from different locations, with some traveling great distances to honor family and friends who have died. After the fire fades, the ashes from their loved ones will be covered with soil that is piled up into a hill, like the mound you see over there."

"That mound is tall!" squeaked Squirrel.

"Yes indeed, it is over 15 feet tall, which is equal to about 20 squirrels standing on top of one another," explained Owl.

"How do the people from distant lands get here?" questioned Rabbit.

"As I fly and explore along the river, watching the beavers build their lodge or the great blue heron grab a fish, I often see people docking their dugout canoes along the river bank. They carry ornaments in their hands and file up to the entrance of this sacred mound space."

"Let's journey down to the river to see if others are coming to the ceremony."

Owl took flight. Rabbit and Squirrel scurried to keep up as they headed towards the river. Hopping through the woods and fields created a temptation to stop and nibble on a walnut or a tender goosefoot leaf, but if they stopped too long, a predator might nibble on them! Knowing that Owl was flying overhead providing protection for her friends, Rabbit and Squirrel scampered along to catch a glimpse of what was happening.

At the river, Squirrel, Owl, and Rabbit met up with Duck and Frog who were hidden in amongst the brush. Together they all stared at the many people climbing out of their dugout canoes, carrying sacred items that were unknown to the animals. Obsidian spear points were brought from Wyoming. Coming from North Carolina was a carved mica hand wrapped in deerskin. The people from Florida donned shark teeth necklaces. A man from the Lake Superior region wore an earspool in each ear and a copper breastplate decorated with four raptors. Owl puffed up proudly to see another bird of prey etched on this breastplate.

"It appears that many arrived by canoe," said Squirrel, "but is it possible to travel by water from such far off lands?"

Duck quacked enthusiastically, "I can answer that. No one knows watersheds quite like a duck. With Mound City and other Hopewell sites being located along rivers, such as the Scioto River, water transportation is ideal. The guests traveling from Wyoming came the longest distance, almost 2000 miles.

Their river journey started on the Yellowstone River, which then joined the Missouri River. From there they rode on the Mississippi River, to the Ohio, and finally up the Scioto River."

"Are there other ways to travel here?" Squirrel wanted to know.

"Yes, some are arriving on foot," Owl responded. "But for now, let's follow these river people up to the ceremonies. Then maybe we can catch a glimpse of others arriving and discover the footpaths they walked and the ceremonial gifts they bring."

Squirrel, Rabbit, Duck, and Frog scampered up the bank with Beaver and Otter joining the crowd. Sprinting as quickly as their little legs would carry them, they shadowed the villagers approaching the ceremonial grounds. As Owl had suggested, they discovered more travelers arriving, but coming by foot.

Beaver looked up at Owl, "Can you see the path those villagers took?"

"Yes," replied Owl. "As I fly high in the sky, I often observe people traveling to our ceremonial mounds here at Mound City from the geometrically shaped ones at Newark Earthworks. These Hopewell people know their geometry. They use geometric shapes, such as squares, rectangles, circles, and octagons, to design many of the mound sites. I have seen their mounds throughout Ohio; many mounds of the same shapes, sizes, and designs."

Otter clutched a fish in his mouth, dropped this gift at the base of the mound, and eyed the many objects lying about. "Look at those rainbow colored rocks. Where did they find those unusual stones? I have never seen outcroppings like this along the Scioto River."

"You would be amazed at the beautiful rocks that are dug out by the Hopewell at Flint Ridge, a quarry filled with colorful flint, which is near the Newark Earthworks," Owl proudly exclaimed. She was enjoying having this chance to share her findings from flying over 60 miles north of Chillicothe to visit these geometric earthworks.

Otter, still distracted by the colorful flint, added his observations. "It looks like the flint has been shaped into tools, such as spear heads and hammer stones. I wonder how these were made."

Owl educated her friends on the fine art of flintknapping. "A flintknapper is a person who knaps flint, shaping the stones into tools; tools like hammerstones for pounding and grinding; large blades for scraping and preparing hides; and spear heads for attaching to the wooden shafts that the hunters then hurl with their atlatls.

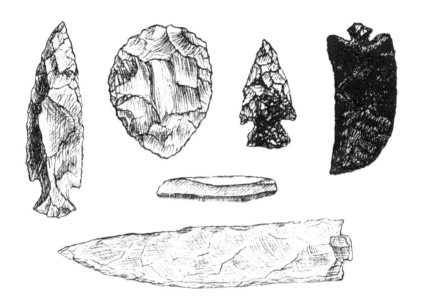

"The flintknapper is one of the many skilled crafts people in the Hopewell culture who creates objects that will outlive them. Sometimes master flintknappers shape tools that are so beautiful that they resemble works of art! These objects are artifacts that may be used to tell future generations about the societies from AD100 who did not record their histories. Without written documents, historians will develop theories and will interpret the culture through the products crafted by these Hopewell artisans - baskets, mounds, jewelry, pottery, breastplates, and pipes."

When Frog heard Owl mention the pipes, she blurted out, "I have seen some of these pipes being used during ceremonies like the one today. Many of them depict us. Otter, your carving shows you holding a fish. And Rabbit, you look like you are ready to hop."

Owl, recollecting her journeys along the rivers, explained, "I have found lots of animal pipes used by the other communities. Dogs, wolves, mountain lions, raccoons, great blue herons, ravens, crows, and hawks were carved. These animals are ones that the Hopewell and I have seen playing in the woods and fields.

All of us here – Rabbit, Squirrel, Otter with his fish, Duck, Frog, Beaver - can be found on pipes."

The animals smiled to know that they were part of this history. THUMP, THUD, THUMP. The sounds of the drum brought their thoughts back to the present, and they began their own version of the Hopewell ceremony, dancing and waddling at the edge of the mound.

GLOSSARY

"**AD**" – "AD" comes from the Latin "Anno Domini", which translates to the year of our Lord. In the Christian tradition, "AD" includes times since Christ was born.

Artifacts – Artifacts are objects made by human hands. The surviving Hopewell Culture artifacts provide clues that enable people of the 21st-century to learn more about this past culture.

Atlatl – Atlatls are tools used for throwing spears. The atlatl allowed the Hopewell to throw a spear much farther and harder than if thrown by hand.

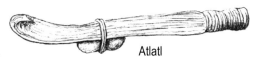
Atlatl

Baskets – While organic material is less likely to survive, evidence of baskets has appeared on the mound surfaces, indicating that baskets were used to carry dirt to build these earthworks. It is estimated that more than 7 million cubic feet of earth was moved to build Newark Earthworks.

Breastplates – The Hopewell breastplates were worn as decoration on the body and were made of copper shaped into rectangles, often including ornamental cutouts such as birds. The copper used for these breastplates came mostly from the Lake Superior region.

Ceremony – Ceremonies are formal, established rituals of observance that often are for religious or sacred events.

Dugout Canoes – Dugout canoes, also known as log boats, are one of the simplest and earliest forms of water transportation. They were made by hollowing out a fallen tree through the use of burning with fire and then scraping out the charred wood.

Dugout Canoe

Earthworks – The Hopewell Culture is known for the art and artifacts that they created. The earthworks are an example of structures or architecture made predominantly of earth and sometimes with stone facings. Many shapes and types were created, such as earthen mounds, earthen walls, and ditches. The earthworks of the Hopewell were often formed into geometric shapes.

Effigy – An effigy is an image or shape that represents a person or animal.

Flint – Flint is a hard rock that is flaked or knapped to form tools and weapons. The flint from the Flint Ridge Quarries in Brownsville, Ohio was valued for its rainbow colors.

Flintknapper – A flintknapper is a person who chips or knaps away pieces of the flint to shape tools and weapons.

Foods – The Hopewell ate the foods that were available naturally, such as nuts, fruits, berries, and animals. Walnut, hickory, and pawpaw trees and wild berries, such as black raspberries, continue to grow abundantly in the areas where the Hopewell lived.

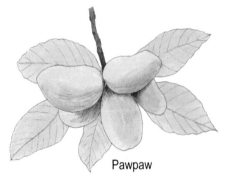

Pawpaw

They also grew some domesticated plants, such as squash, sunflower and goosefoot.

Goosefoot – Goosefoot, now extinct, was a native plant that the Hopewell used for food. Its seeds matured in the fall and were eaten as a source of protein and fiber. They could be ground to make a meal or boiled until soft to make a cereal.

Goosefoot

Hammerstones – A hammerstone is a stone tool used as a hammer for activities such as chipping flint, grinding food, or breaking up bones.

Hammerstone

Hopewell Culture – Ohio's prehistoric cultures were named for the location where artifacts were first recognized as the works of a distinct culture. The Hopewell objects date between AD 1 to 400. These objects, similar in style, were first recognized as the works of a distinct culture at the Hopewell Mound Group. The Hopewell Mound Group was located on Mordecai Hopewell's land in Ross County, Ohio.

Mica – Mica, which is composed of crystallized minerals that form thin and translucent layers, was brought to Ohio from the Blue Ridge Mountains of North Carolina. It was found in the Hopewell mounds in sheets, as well as shaped into designs, such as the mica hand and the eagle's claw.

Mica Hand

Mounds – A mound is a pile or bank of earth that often covers a ceremonial structure or burial.

Obsidian – Obsidian, a hard, volcanic glass found in the Rocky Mountain area, was used to create symbolic artifacts.

Pipes – The Hopewell made pipes that were both plain and shaped into effigies. The pipes were made from pipestone found in Ohio, Indiana, and Illinois and were used to smoke native tobacco.

Frog Effigy Pipe

Prehistory – Prehistory represents a period of time before the presence of written records. This is the definition used by historians and archaeologists and is the definition used for this book. While no written records have been found for the Hopewell Culture, its surviving artifacts provide a look into the history of these early people.

Spear Points   A spear point is a sharp blade that is attached to a spear and used for hunting.

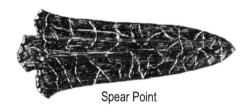
Spear Point

MOUNDS IN OHIO

It has been estimated that at one point in time the total number of earthworks was more than 11,000. In 1914, William C. Mills used earlier maps created by Warren K. Moorehead, Lucy Allen, Charles Whittlesey and the Smithsonian Institution to examine each Ohio county in order to update and create a master map, indicating the vast number of mounds. The majority of these mounds were located in southern Ohio in what is today Scioto, Ross, Pickaway, Butler, Hamilton, Warren, Washington, and Licking Counties. Over the years, farming and development have eroded or destroyed many of these mounds. Many surviving earthworks are protected by private organizations, as well as federal and state agencies. Eight Ohio earthwork sites are currently (2019) proposed for UNESCO's World Heritage List, the highest designation possible for a cultural or natural site.

HOPEWELL SITES IN OHIO

The Earthworks at Newark Ohio (built by the Ohio Hopewell Culture between ca. AD 1 to 400) include the 1200 –foot-diameter Great Circle with its steep inner ditch and monumental framed gateway, plus the Octagon Earthworks – a perfect circle and adjoining octagon over a half-mile across – whose eye-level embankments align with all eight of the key rise- and set-points of the moon during its 18.6-year cycle, within a smaller margin of error than that at Stonehenge. Another surviving piece of the once-vast Newark complex is a corner of the square, now the Wright Earthworks. www.ohiohistory.org/visit/museum-and-site-locator/newark-earthworks

Flint Ridge Ancient Quarries and Nature Preserve is known as the "Great Indian Quarry of Ohio" and is found in eastern Ohio. Flint Ridge flint has been quarried for over 12,000 years. It was and continues to be valued for its bright colors, including red, pink, yellow, blue, and green. The Hopewell people especially prized it and used it to make small knives and bladelets.

www.ohiohistorycentral.org/w/Flint_Ridge

The Fort Ancient Hilltop Enclosure sits above a narrow gorge of the Little Miami River and includes three-and-a-half miles of sinuous earthen embankments that are accompanied by a continuous necklace of clay-lined ponds. The enclosure has 67 gates.

www.ohiohistory.org/visit/museum-and-site-locator/fort-ancient-earthworks

High Bank Earthworks is the only other circle-octagon combination built by the Hopewell, besides the Earthworks at Newark. Like at Newark, the rise and set points of the moon are marked by key alignments. The sun's cycles are also encoded at High Bank Earthworks. www.nps.gov/hocu/learn/historyculture/high-bank-works.htm

Hopeton Earthworks is located about one mile east and across the Scioto River from the Mound City Group. The 292 acre site contains a square enclosure that is joined to a circle, with smaller circular structures joining the square. www.nps.gov/hocu/learn/historyculture/hopeton-earthworks.htm

Hopewell Culture National Historical Park includes geometric enclosures near Chillicothe, Ohio (headquarters at Mound City) that are the most spectacular concentration of such sites and illustrate subtle spatial variations of the arrangement of mounds and enclosing squares and circles. These mounds have yielded some of the most outstanding art objects produced in pre-Columbian North America. Many were made from raw materials (such as mica and obsidian) brought to Ohio from locations throughout the US, suggesting that these Hopewell sites were important ceremonial centers for much of the continent. Sites to visit include – Mound City, Hopewell Mound Group, Seip Earthworks, Hopeton Earthworks, & High Bank Earthworks.
www.nps.gov/hocu/index.htm

Hopewell Mound Group was first excavated in the 1890s. It became the type site for the Hopewell Culture, with the spectacular artifacts discovered in its several mounds, giving its owner's name (Mordecai Hopewell) to the whole culture. www.nps.gov/hocu/learn/historyculture/hopewell-mound-group.htm

Mound City Group is the largest concentration of burial mounds in the Hopewell Culture, with a collection of two dozen mounds that cover the remains of funerary buildings. It is enclosed by a low wall in the shape of a square with rounded corners. It is the headquarters for the Hopewell Culture National Historical Park. www.nps.gov/hocu/learn/historyculture/mound-city-group.htm

Seip Earthworks is located along Paint Creek. It is one of two dozen geometric earthwork complexes constructed in the Paint Creek and Scioto River valleys. Seip Earthworks originally contained one immense circle, a smaller circle, and a 27 acre square with astronomical alignments. Today's remaining large mound covered the remains of a ceremonial building. www.nps.gov/hocu/learn/historyculture/seip-earthworks.htm

More detailed information about the Hopewell, the Hopewell Culture and the Ohio Hopewell UNESCO World Heritage sites can be found in these reference sources:

Guide to the Hopewell Ceremonial Earthworks. Eight Ancient American Indian Monuments Being Prepared for UNESCO World Heritage, Columbus, Ohio. 2019

Hopewell Culture National Historical Park. Expeditions into Ohio's Past – Teacher's Guide, An Integrated Curriculum for Grades 3-5. Chillicothe, Ohio. 2008

Lepper, Bradley T. Ohio Archaeology-An Illustrated Chronicle of Ohio's Ancient American Indian Cultures. Wilmington, Ohio. 2005

Acknowledgments

I am indebted to the many people who helped make *A Bird's Eye View of the Hopewell* become a reality. I am grateful to the guidance from staff members at the Ohio History Connection, including Todd Kleismit and Jennifer Aultman, and especially to Brad Lepper who was always willing to proof the manuscript and to share his vast knowledge about the Hopewell Culture. Their desire, along with the Hopewell Culture National Historical Park, to honor these sites through a UNESCO World Heritage nomination reflects the pride and respect for their beauty and cultural significance. Marnie Leist, Ben Barnes, and Christine Morris provided valuable insights and an educational awareness about the Native American perspectives on the Hopewell. Kati Aitken created the book's accompanying block print and pen and ink illustrations. Her talents are seen in many areas, from her artistic skills, to her desire for accuracy, to her willingness to work as a team. My fourth grade students at Columbus School for Girls, along with my teaching partner Tracy Kessler, always kept history alive as we worked together to explore the ancient Ohio cultures, traveled on field trips to Ohio's prehistoric locations, and spent several years working with the Ohio History Connection to make the Adena Pipe Ohio's official state artifact. Lois Tynan has provided continual encouragement and a children's librarian's editing eye, while Aaron Keirns shared his artistic skills to weave all of the book parts together for publication.

My family has always shared a love of history. Early on, my mother and father created an interest in the past, by exploring different historical museums during weekends and on family vacations. Dinner conversations often revolved around historic and current events. My grandmother, Mary Baum Knisley, who grew up on the Baum prehistoric site in Ross County, Ohio, recounted stories to me about the archaeologist who explored the Baum site in the early 1900s, and together we often visited the Ohio History Center to see some of the artifacts that were collected from her family farm. She was proud that her dad wanted to preserve the significance of the land's history, as well as discover more about the early Ohioans who had lived there a couple centuries ago. My husband has played a key role in encouraging the idea of the picture book. He always is ready for exploring mounds or other prehistoric sites, and he shares the joy of absorbing the space while respecting the beauty and mystery these prehistoric Ohioans left for future generations.

Author's Note

With over 30 years of teaching Ohio history to elementary students, I yearned for a picture book that provided an overall view of the prehistoric people who lived thousands of years ago in the area now known as Ohio. *A Bird's Eye View of the Hopewell* was written to fill that niche, providing a picture book that brings to life the Hopewell Culture, one of several different cultural periods that have been identified in prehistoric Ohio.

While the true names of these different cultures are unknown, modern archaeologists have assigned them ones that relate to where many similarly styled artifacts were first discovered. The Hopewell Culture's name came from a Ross County farm owned by Mordecai Hopewell. As a prehistoric culture, the Hopewell did not leave any written records, but they did leave a vast wealth of artifacts – jewelry, effigy pipes, breastplates, spear points, pottery – to name a few. Through these surviving artifacts, through archaeological digs, and through the study of connections to other cultures, archaeologists have developed theories about how the Hopewell may have lived. *A Bird's Eye View of the Hopewell* is an attempt to weave together these theories into a fictional story that children and adults can relate to.

Author & Illustrator Biographies

Charlotte Stiverson taught in classrooms and museums for over 35 years, with 25 years teaching Ohio history to fourth graders. Recently retired, she continues to educate through workshops. *A Bird's Eye View of the Hopewell* is her second book. Her first book, *Nellie's Walk*, won a Grand Award in the 2017 APEX Awards for Publication Excellence. Charlotte enjoys nature, history, art, and spending time with her family and friends. She currently lives in the woods of southwestern Ohio (Hopewell country) with her husband and cat.

Kati Aitken is a freelance artist/illustrator who always has loved animal stories and the legends of the Native Americans. These legends have much of the same magic as the stories of the Sámi people who live in the north of Kati's native Finland. Kati has illustrated numerous picture books, with many of her works focused on animals, people, and nature. She uses a variety of media - watercolour, oil, printmaking, ink/wash, and charcoal - with blockprinting and ink/wash being incorporated into her illustrations for *A Bird's Eye View of the Hopewell*.

Made in the USA
Middletown, DE
21 July 2022